Absalom and Achitophel. A poem. Written by Mr. Dryden. To which is added an explanatory key never printed before.

John Dryden

Eighteenth Century
Collections Online
Print Editions

Gale ECCO Print Editions

Relive history with *Eighteenth Century Collections Online*, now available in print for the independent historian and collector. This series includes the most significant English-language and foreign-language works printed in Great Britain during the eighteenth century, and is organized in seven different subject areas including literature and language; medicine, science, and technology; and religion and philosophy. The collection also includes thousands of important works from the Americas.

The eighteenth century has been called "The Age of Enlightenment." It was a period of rapid advance in print culture and publishing, in world exploration, and in the rapid growth of science and technology – all of which had a profound impact on the political and cultural landscape. At the end of the century the American Revolution, French Revolution and Industrial Revolution, perhaps three of the most significant events in modern history, set in motion developments that eventually dominated world political, economic, and social life.

In a groundbreaking effort, Gale initiated a revolution of its own: digitization of epic proportions to preserve these invaluable works in the largest online archive of its kind. Contributions from major world libraries constitute over 175,000 original printed works. Scanned images of the actual pages, rather than transcriptions, recreate the works *as they first appeared.*

Now for the first time, these high-quality digital scans of original works are available via print-on-demand, making them readily accessible to libraries, students, independent scholars, and readers of all ages.

For our initial release we have created seven robust collections to form one the world's most comprehensive catalogs of 18th century works.

Initial Gale ECCO Print Editions collections include:

History and Geography
Rich in titles on English life and social history, this collection spans the world as it was known to eighteenth-century historians and explorers. Titles include a wealth of travel accounts and diaries, histories of nations from throughout the world, and maps and charts of a world that was still being discovered. Students of the War of American Independence will find fascinating accounts from the British side of conflict.

Social Science

Delve into what it was like to live during the eighteenth century by reading the first-hand accounts of everyday people, including city dwellers and farmers, businessmen and bankers, artisans and merchants, artists and their patrons, politicians and their constituents. Original texts make the American, French, and Industrial revolutions vividly contemporary.

Medicine, Science and Technology

Medical theory and practice of the 1700s developed rapidly, as is evidenced by the extensive collection, which includes descriptions of diseases, their conditions, and treatments. Books on science and technology, agriculture, military technology, natural philosophy, even cookbooks, are all contained here.

Literature and Language

Western literary study flows out of eighteenth-century works by Alexander Pope, Daniel Defoe, Henry Fielding, Frances Burney, Denis Diderot, Johann Gottfried Herder, Johann Wolfgang von Goethe, and others. Experience the birth of the modern novel, or compare the development of language using dictionaries and grammar discourses.

Religion and Philosophy

The Age of Enlightenment profoundly enriched religious and philosophical understanding and continues to influence present-day thinking. Works collected here include masterpieces by David Hume, Immanuel Kant, and Jean-Jacques Rousseau, as well as religious sermons and moral debates on the issues of the day, such as the slave trade. The Age of Reason saw conflict between Protestantism and Catholicism transformed into one between faith and logic -- a debate that continues in the twenty-first century.

Law and Reference

This collection reveals the history of English common law and Empire law in a vastly changing world of British expansion. Dominating the legal field is the *Commentaries of the Law of England* by Sir William Blackstone, which first appeared in 1765. Reference works such as almanacs and catalogues continue to educate us by revealing the day-to-day workings of society.

Fine Arts

The eighteenth-century fascination with Greek and Roman antiquity followed the systematic excavation of the ruins at Pompeii and Herculaneum in southern Italy; and after 1750 a neoclassical style dominated all artistic fields. The titles here trace developments in mostly English-language works on painting, sculpture, architecture, music, theater, and other disciplines. Instructional works on musical instruments, catalogs of art objects, comic operas, and more are also included.

The BiblioLife Network

This project was made possible in part by the BiblioLife Network (BLN), a project aimed at addressing some of the huge challenges facing book preservationists around the world. The BLN includes libraries, library networks, archives, subject matter experts, online communities and library service providers. We believe every book ever published should be available as a high-quality print reproduction; printed on-demand anywhere in the world. This insures the ongoing accessibility of the content and helps generate sustainable revenue for the libraries and organizations that work to preserve these important materials.

The following book is in the "public domain" and represents an authentic reproduction of the text as printed by the original publisher. While we have attempted to accurately maintain the integrity of the original work, there are sometimes problems with the original work or the micro-film from which the books were digitized. This can result in minor errors in reproduction. Possible imperfections include missing and blurred pages, poor pictures, markings and other reproduction issues beyond our control. Because this work is culturally important, we have made it available as part of our commitment to protecting, preserving, and promoting the world's literature.

GUIDE TO FOLD-OUTS MAPS and OVERSIZED IMAGES

The book you are reading was digitized from microfilm captured over the past thirty to forty years. Years after the creation of the original microfilm, the book was converted to digital files and made available in an online database.

In an online database, page images do not need to conform to the size restrictions found in a printed book. When converting these images back into a printed bound book, the page sizes are standardized in ways that maintain the detail of the original. For large images, such as fold-out maps, the original page image is split into two or more pages

Guidelines used to determine how to split the page image follows:

• Some images are split vertically; large images require vertical and horizontal splits.
• For horizontal splits, the content is split left to right.
• For vertical splits, the content is split from top to bottom.
• For both vertical and horizontal splits, the image is processed from top left to bottom right.

ABSALOM

AND

ACHITOPHEL.

A

POEM.

———*Si Proprius ſtes*
Te Capiet Magis———

Written by Mr. DRYDEN.

To which is added an explanatory Key never
Printed before.

Dublin : Printed by *James Hoey,* and *George Faulk-
ner,* at the Pamphlet Shop, oppoſite the *Tholſel*
in *Skinner-Row,* 1729.

ABSALOM

To the unknown Author of this admirable POEM.

I Thought, forgive my Sin, the boasted fire
   Of Poets Souls did long ago expire ;
   Of Folly or of Madness did accuse
The wretch that thought himself possest with Muse;
Laugh'd at the God within, that did inspire
With more than human thoughts the tuneful Quire;
But sure 'tis more than Fancy, or a Dream
Of Rhimers slumbring by the Muses stream,
Some livelier Spark of Heav'n, and more refin'd
From Earthly dross, fills the great Poet's Mind.
Witness these mighty and immortal Lines,
Through each of which th' informing Genius shines·
Scarce a diviner Flame inspir'd the King
Of whom thy Muse does so sublimely sing.
Not *David*'s self could in a nobler Verse
His gloriously offending Son rehearse,
Tho' in his Breast the Prophet's Fury met,
The Father's Fondness, and the Poet's Wit.
   Here all consent in Wonder and in Praise,
And to the Unknown Poet Altars raise.
Which thou must needs accept with equal joy,
As when *Æneas* heard the Wars of *Troy*,
Wrapt up himself in darkness and unseen,
Extoll'd with Wonder by the *Tyrian* Queen.
Sure thou already art secure of Fame,
Nor want'st new Glories to exalt thy Name:
What Father else could have refus'd to own
So great a Son as God-like *Absalom.*

ABSALOM

ABSALOM
AND
ACHITOPHEL.

A
POEM.

IN pious Times, e'er Prieſt-craft did begin,
Before *Polygamy* was made a Sin;
When Man on many multiply'd his kind,
E'er one to one was curſedly confin'd:
When Nature prompted, and no Law deny'd
Promiſcuous uſe of Concubine and Bride;
Then, *Iſrael*'s Monarch, after Heaven's own heart,
His vigorous warmth did variouſly impart
To Wives and Slaves; and, wide as his Command,
Scatter'd his Maker's Image, through the Land.
Michal, of Royal Blood, the Crown did wear;
A Soil ungrateful to the Tiller's care:
Not ſo the reſt; for ſeveral Mothers bore
To God-like *David*, ſeveral Sons before.
But, ſince like Slaves his Bed they did aſcend,
No true Succeſſion cou'd their Seed attend,
Of all the numerous Progeny was none
So Beautiful, ſo Brave as *Abſalom*:
Whether, inſpir'd by ſome diviner Luſt,
His Father got him with a greater Guſt;

Or

Or that his conſcious Deſtiny made way,
By Manly Beauty to Imperial Sway;
Early in foreign Fields he won Renown,
With Kings and States Ally'd to *Iſrael*'s Crown:
In Peace the thoughts of War he could remove,
And ſeem'd as he were only born for Love.
Whate'er he did, was done with ſo much eaſe,
In him alone, 'twas Natural to pleaſe:
His motions all Accompany'd with grace;
And *Paradiſe* was open'd in his face.
With ſecret Joy, indulgent *David* view'd:
His youthful Image in his Son renew'd:
To all his wiſhes nothing he deny'd;
And made the Charming *Annabel* his Bride.
What faults he had (for who from faults is free?)
His Father cou'd not, or he wou'd not ſee.
Some warm exceſſes, which the Law forbore,
Were conſtru'd Youth that purg'd by boyling o'er:
And *Ammon*'s Mother by a ſpecious Name,
Was call'd a juſt Revenge for injur'd Fame.
Thus prais'd, and lov'd, the noble Youth remain'd,
While *David* undiſturb'd in *Sion* reign'd.
But Life can never be ſincerely bleſt:
Heav'n puniſhes the bad, and proves the beſt.
The *Jews* a Head-ſtrong, Moody Murm'ring race,
As ever try'd th' extent and ſtretch of Grace;
God's pamper'd People whom, debauch'd with eaſe,
No King cou'd govern, nor no God cou'd pleaſe;
(Gods they had try'd of every Shape and Size,
That God-ſmiths cou'd produce, or Prieſts deviſe.)
Theſe *Adam*-wits too fortunately free,
Began to dream they wanted Liberty,

And

And when no rule, no preſident was found,
Of Men by Laws leſs circumſcrib'd and bound;
They led their wild deſires to Woods and Caves;
And thought that all but Savages were Slaves.
They who when *Saul* was dead without a blow,
Made fooliſh *Iſhboſheth* the Crown forego;
Who baniſh'd *David* did from *Hebron* bring,
And, with a general Shout proclaim'd him King:
Thoſe very *Jews*, who at their very beſt,
Their Humours more than Loyalty expreſt,
Now, wonder why, ſo long, they had obey'd
An Idol-Monarch which their Hands had made:
Thought they might ruin him they cou'd create;
Or melt him to that Golden Calf, a State.
But theſe were random bolts: Not form'd Deſign,
Nor Intereſt made the Factious Croud to join;
The ſober part of *Iſrael*, free from Stain,
Well knew the value of a peaceful Reign;
And looking backward with a wiſe afright,
Saw Seams of Wounds, diſhoneſt to the Sight;
In contemplation of whoſe ugly Scars,
They curſt the Memory of Civil Wars.
The moderate ſort of Men, thus qualiſi'd,
Inclin'd the Ballance to the better ſide:
And *David*'s mildneſs manag'd it ſo well,
The bad found no occaſion to Rebel.
But when to Sin our byaſt Nature leans,
The careful Devil is ſtill at hand with means;
And providently Pimps for ill deſires;
The Good Old Cauſe reviv'd, a Plot requires.
Plots true or falſe, are neceſſary things,
To raiſe up Common-wealths, and ruin Kings.

The

The Inhabitants of Old *Jeruſalem*
Were *Jebuſites* : the Town ſo call'd from them ;
And their's the Native right————
But when the choſen People grew more ſtrong,
The rightful Cauſe at length became the wrong
And every loſs the Men of *Jebus* bore,
They ſtill were thought God's Enemies the more.
Thus worn and weaken'd well or ill content,
Submit they muſt to *David*'s Government :
Impoveriſht and depriv'd of all Command,
Their Taxes doubled as they loſt their Land ;
And what was harder yet to fleſh and blood,
Their Gods diſgrac'd, and burnt like common Woo
This ſet the Heathen Prieſt-hood in a flame ;
For Prieſts of all Religions are the ſame :
Of whatſoe'er deſcent their God-head be,
Stock, Stone, or other homely Pedigree,
In his defence his Servants are as bold,
As if he had been born of beaten Gold,
The *Jewiſh Rabbins,* thought their Enemies,
In this conclude them honeſt Men and wiſe :
For 'twas their Duty, all the Learned think,
T' eſpouſe his Cauſe by whom they eat and drin
From hence began that Plot, the Nation's Curſe
Bad in its ſelf, but repreſented worſe.
Rais'd in extremes, and in extremes decry'd ;
With Oaths affirm'd, with dying Vows deny'd.
Not weigh'd, or winnow'd by the Multitude ;
But ſwallow'd in the Maſs, unchew'd and crude
Some truth there was, but daſht and brew'd w
To pleaſe the Fools, and puzzle all the Wiſe.   (L
Succeeding Times did equal Folly call,
Believing nothing, or believing all.

Th' *Ægyptian* Rights the *Jebuſites* embrac'd ;
Where Gods were recommended by their taſte:
Such Sav'ry Deities muſt needs be good,
As ſerv'd at once for Worſhip and for Food.
By force they could not introduce theſe Gods ;
For Ten to One in former Days was odds.
So Fraud was us'd, (the Sacrificer's Trade,)
Fools are more hard to conquer than perſuade.
Their buſie Teachers mingled with the *Jews* ;
And rak'd for Converts, even the Court and Stews :
Which *Hebrew Prieſts* the more unkindly took,
Becauſe the Fleece accompanies the Flock.
Some thought they God's anointed meant to ſlay
By Guns, invented ſince full many a day :
Our Author Swears it not ; but who can know
How far the Devil and *Jebuſites* may go ?
This *Plot* which fail'd for want of common Senſe,
Had yet a deep and dangerousConſequence :
For as when raging Fevers boil the Blood,
The ſtanding Lakes ſoon float into a Flood ;
And ev'ry Hoſtile Humour ; which before
ſlept quiet in itsChannels bubbles o'er :
ſo ſeveral Factions from this firſt Ferment,
Work up to Foam, and threat the Government.
ſome by their Friends, more by themſelves thought
ſuppos'd thePow'r, to which they could not riſe,(wiſe,
ſome had in Courts been great, and thrown from
likeFriends were harden'd in Impenitence. (thence,
ſome by their Monarch's fatal mercy grown
from pardon'd Rebels, Kinſmen to the Throne ;
Were rais'd in Pow'r and publick Office high :
Strong Bands, if Bands ungrateful Men cou'd tye.

Of thefe the falfe *Achitophel* was firft;
A Name to all fucceeding Ages curft.
For clofe Defigns, and crooked Counfels fit;
Sagacious, Bold, and Turbulent of Wit:
Reftlefs, unfixt in Principles and Place;
In Pow'r unpleas'd, impatient of Difgrace.
A fiery Soul, which working out its way,
Fretted the Pigmy Body to decay;
And o'er inform'd the Tenement of Clay.
A daring Pilot in extremity;   (high
Pleas'd with the Danger, when the Waves went
He fought the Storms: but for a Calm unfit;
Would fteer too nigh the Sands, to boaft his Wit.
Great Wits are fure to Madnefs near ally'd;
And thin partitions do their Bounds divide;
Elfe, why fhould he, with wealth and honour bleft
Refufe his Age the needful Hours of Reft?
Punifh a Body which he cou'd not pleafe;
Bankrupt of Life, yet Prodigal of eafe?
And all to leave, what with his Toil he won,
To that unfeather'd two legg'd thing, a Son:
Got, while his Soul did huddl'd Notions try;
And born a fhapelefs Lump, like Anarchy.
In Friendfhip falfe, implacable in Hate:
Refolv'd to Ruin or to Rule the State,
To Compafs this, the Triple Bond he broke;
The Pillars of the Publick fafety fhook:
And fitted *Ifrael* for a Foreign Yoke.
Then, feiz'd with Fear, yet ftill affecting Fame
Ufurp'd a Patriot's All attoning Name.
So eafie ftill it proves in Factious Times,
With publick Zeal to cancel private Crimes:

How

How ſafe is Treaſon, and how ſacred Ill,
Where none can Sin againſt the Peoples Will?
Where Crouds can wink; and no offence be known
Since in another's guilt they find their own.
Yet. Fame deſerv'd, no Enemy can grudge ;
The Stateſman we abhor, but praiſe the Judge.
In *Iſrael's* Courts ne'er ſat an *Abbethdin*
With more diſcerning Eyes, or Hands more clean;
Unbrib'd, unſought, the Wretched to redreſs ;
Swift of Diſpatch and eaſie of Acceſs.
Oh, had he been content to ſerve the Crown,
With Virtues only proper to the Gown ;
Or, had the rankneſs of the Soil been freed,
From Cockle, that oppreſt the Noble Seed:
David. for him his tuneful Harp had ſtrung,
And Heav'n had wanted one Immortal Song.
But wild Ambition loves to ſlide, not ſtand ;
And Fortunes Ice prefers to Virtues Land,
Achitophel, grown weary to poſſeſs
A lawful Fame, and lazy Happineſs ;
Diſdain'd the Golden Fruit to gather free,
And lent the Croud his Arm to ſhake the Tree,
Now manifeſt of Crimes, contriv'd long ſince,
He ſtood at bold Defiance with his Prince ;
Held up the Buckler of the Peoples Cauſe,
Againſt the Crown ; and ſculk'd behind the Laws.
The wiſh'd occaſion of the Plot he takes;
Some Circumſtances finds, but more he makes,
By buzzing Emiſſaries, fills the Ears
Of liſtning Crouds, with Jealouſies and Fears,
Of Arbitrary Counſels brought to light,
And proves the King himſelf a *Jebuſite*.

Weak

Weak Arguments! which yet he knew full well,
Were ftrong with people eafie to Rebel:
For, govern'd by the *Moon*, the giddy *Jews*
Tread the fame Track when fhe the Prime renews:
And once in twenty years, their Scribes Record,
By natural Inftinct they change their Lord,
Achitophel ftill wants a Chief and none
Was found fo fit as War-like *Abfalom*:
Not, that he wifh'd his Greatnefs to create,
(For Politicians neither love nor hate:)
But, for he knew, his Title not allow'd,
Would keep him ftill depending on the Croud:
That Kingly Pow'r, thus ebbing out, might be
Drawn to the Dregs of a Democracy.
Him he attempts, with Studied Arts to pleafe,
And fheds his Venome, in fuch words as thefe.
   Aufpicious Prince, at whofe Nativity
Some Royal Planet rul'd the Southern Sky;
Thy longing Countries Darling and Defire;
Their cloudy Pillar, and their guardian Fire;
Their fecond *Mofes*, whofe extended Wand
Divides the Seas, and fhews the promis'd Land
Whofe dawning Day, in every diftant Age,
Has exercis'd the Sacred Prophet's rage:
The Peoples Pray'r, the glad Diviner's Theme,
The Young mens Vifion, and the Old mens Dream!
Thee *Saviour*, Thee, the Nations Vows confefs;
And never Satisfi'd with feeing, blefs;
Swift, unbefpoken Pomps, thy fteps proclaim,
And ftammering Babes are taught to lifp thy Name.
How long wilt thou the general Joy detain;
Starve, and defraud the People of thy Reign?
                    Content

Content ingloriouſly to paſs thy Days
Like one of Virtues Fools that feeds on Praiſe;
Till thy freſh Glories, which now ſhine ſo bright,
Grow ſtale and Tarniſh with our daily ſight.
B'lieve me, Royal Youth, thy Fruit muſt be,
Or gather'd ripe, or rot upon the Tree.
Heav'n has to all allotted, ſoon or late,
Some lucky Revolution of their Fate.
Whoſe Motions, if we watch and guide with Skill,
(For humane Good depends on humane Will,)
Our Fortune rolls us from a ſmooth Deſcent,
And, from the firſt Impreſſion, takes the Bent.
But, if unſeiz'd, ſhe glides away like wind;
And leaves repenting Folly far behind.
Now, now ſhe meets you with a glorious prize,
And ſpreads her locks before her as ſhe flyes.
Had thus old *David*, from whoſe Loins you Spring,
Not dar'd, when Fortune call'd him to be King,
At *Gath* an Exile he might ſtill remain;
And Heav'ns Anointing Oyl had been in vain.
Let his ſucceſsful Youth your hopes engage;
But ſhun th' example of declining Age.
Behold him ſetting in his Weſtern Skyes,
The ſhadows lengthning as the Vapours riſe.
He is not now, as when in *Jordan*'s Sand,
The Joyful People throng'd to ſee him Land,
Cov'ring the *Beech*, and blackning all the *Strand*:
But, like the Prince of Angels from his height,
Comes tumbling downward with diminiſh'd Light;
Betray'd by one poor Plot to publick Scorn;
(Our only Bleſſing ſince his curſt Return)
Theſe heaps of People which one Sheaf did bind,
Blown off, and ſcatter'd by a Puff of Wind.

What

What Strength can he to your Defigns oppofe,
Naked of Friends and round befet with Foes ?
If *Pharoah's* doubtful fuccour he fhould ufe,
A Foreign Aid would more incenfe the *Jews* :
Proud *Ægypt* wou'd diffembled Friendfhip bring;
Foment the War, but not fupport the King;
Nor wou'd the Royal Party e'er unite,
With *Pharoah's* Arms, t' affift the *Jebufite* ;
Or if they fhou'd, their Intereft foon would break
And with fuch odious Aid make *David* weak.
All forts of Men, by my fuccefsful Arts,
Abhorring Kings, eftrange their alter'd Hearts.
From *David's* Rule ; And 'tis their general Cry,
Religion, Common-wealth, and Liberty.
If you as Champion of the Publick Good,
Add to their Arms a Chief of Royal Blood ;
What may not *Ifrael* hope, and what Applaufe,
Might fuch a General gain by fuch a Caufe ?
Not Barren Praife alone, that Gaudy Flow'r,
Fair only to the fight, but folid Pow'r ;
And Nobler is a Limited Command,
Given by the Love of all your Native Land,
Than a Succeffive Title, Long and Dark,
Drawn from the Mouldy Rolls of *Noah's* Ark.
    What cannot Praife effect in mighty minds,
When Flattery fooths, and when Ambition blinds!
Defire of Pow'r, on Earth a Vitious Weed,
Yet, fprung from High, is of Celeftial Seed ;
In God 'tis Glory ; And when Men Afpire,
'Tis but a Spark too much of Heavenly Fire.
Th' Ambitious Youth, too Covetous of Fame,
Too full of Angels Mettal in his Frame ;

Unwarily was led from Virtues ways ;   (Praiſe
Made Drunk with Honour, and Debauch'd with
Half Loath, and half conſenting to the Ill,
(For Royal Blood within him Struggled Still.)
He thus reply'd——And what Pretence have I,
To take up Arms for Publick Liberty ?
My Father Governs with unqueſtion'd Right ;
The Faith's Defender, and Mankinds Delight :
Good, Gracious, Juſt, Obſervant of the Laws ;
And Heav'n by Wonders has eſpous'd his Cauſe.
Whom has he wrong'd in all his Peaceful Reign ?
Who ſues for Juſtice to his Throne in Vain ?
What Millions has he Pardon'd of his Foes,
Whom juſt Revenge did to his Wrath expoſe ?
Mild, Eaſie, Humble, Studious of our Good ;
Inclin'd to Mercy, and averſe from Blood.
If Mildneſs ill with Stubborn *Iſrael* Suit,
His Crime is God's beloved Attribute.
What could he gain, his People to Betray,
Or change his Right, for Arbitrary Sway ?
Let haughty *Pharaoh* Curſe with ſuch a Reign,
His Fruitful *Nile*, and Yoak a Servile Train.
If *David*'s Rule *Jeruſalem* Diſpleaſe,
The *Dog-Star* heats their Brains to this Diſeaſe.
Why then ſhould I Encouraging the Bad,
Turn Rebel, and run Popularly Mad ?
Were he a Tyrant, who, by Lawleſs Might,
Oppreſt the *Jews*, and rais'd the *Jebuſite*,
Well might I Mourn ; but Natures Holy Bands,
Wou'd Curb my Spirits, and reſtrain my Hands :
The People might aſſert their Liberty ;
But what was Right in them, were Crime in me.
                                        His

His Favour leaves me nothing to require;
Prevents my Wiſhes, and out-runs Deſire;
What more can I expect while *David* lives?
All but his Kingly Diadem he gives:
And that: But there he paus'd: then Sighing ſaid,
Is juſtly deſtin'd for a Worthier Head,
For when my Father from his Toyls ſhall Reſt,
And late Augment the Number of the Bleſt;
His Lawful Iſſue ſhall the Throne aſcend;
Or the *Collatr'al* line where that ſhall end.
His Brother, tho' Oppreſt with Vulgar Spight,
Yet Dauntleſs and Secure of Native Right,
Of every Royal Virtue ſtands poſſeſt;
Still dear to all the Braveſt and the Beſt.
His Courage Foes, his Friends his Truth Proclaim;
His Loyalty the King, the World his *Fame.*
His Mercy ev'n th' Offending Croud will find;
For ſure he comes of a Forgiving Kind.
Why ſhould I then Repine at Heaven's Decree;
Which gives me no Pretence to Royalty?
Yet oh that Fate, Propitiouſly Inclin'd,
Had rais'd my Birth, or had debas'd my Mind,
To my large Soul, not all her Treaſure lent,
And then betray'd it to a mean Deſcent.
I find, I find my mounting Spirits Bold,
And *David's* Part diſdains my Mother's Mold.
Why am I ſcanted by a Niggard Birth?
My Soul diſclaims the Kindred of her Earth;
And, made for Empire, whiſpers me within;
Deſire of Greatneſs, is a God-like Sin.

   Him Staggering ſo, when Hell's dire Agent found,
While fainting Virtue ſcarce maintain'd her Ground.

                He

He pours freſh Forces in, and thus Replies :
   Th' Eternal God, ſupremly Good and Wiſe,
Imparts not theſe Prodigious Gifts in vain ;
What wonders are reſerv'd to bleſs your Reign ?
Againſt your Will your Arguments have ſhown,
Such Virtues only given to guide a Throne.
Not that your Father's Mildneſs I contemn ;
But manly Force becomes the Diadem.
'Tis true he grants the People all they crave,
And more perhaps than Subjects ought to have :
For laviſh Grants ſuppoſe a Monarch tame,
And more his Goodneſs than his Wit proclaim;
But when ſhould People ſtrive their Bonds to break,
If not when Kings are Negligent or Weak ?
Let him give on till he can give no more,
The Thrifty Sanhedrin ſhall keep him poor :
And every Sheckle which he can receive,
Shall coſt a Limb of his Prerogative.
To ply him with new Plots, ſhall be my care ;
Or plunge him deep in ſome Expenſive War ;
Which when his Treaſure can no more ſupply,
He muſt, with the Remains of Kingſhip buy
His faithful Friends, our Jealouſies and Fears,
Call *Jebuſites* ; and *Pharoah*'s Penſioners :
Whom, when our Fury from his Aid has torn,
He ſhall be naked left to publick Scorn.
The next Succeſſor, whom I fear and hate,
My Arts have made obnoxious to the State ;
Turn'd all his Virtues to his Overthrow,
And gain'd our Elders to pronounce a Foe.
His Right, for Sums of neceſſary Gold,
Shall firſt be Pawn'd, and afterwards be Sold :
                                    Till

Till time ſhall Ever-wanting *David* draw,
To paſs your doubtful Title into Law:
If not; the People have a Right Supreme
To make their Kings; for Kings are made for them.
All Empire is no more than Pow'r in Truſt;
Which when reſum'd, can be no longer Juſt,
Succeſſion, for the general Good deſign'd,
In its own wrong a Nation cannot bind:
If altering that, the People can relieve,
Better one ſuffer than a Nation grieve,   (choſe,
The *Jews* well knew their Pow'r: e'er *Saul* they
God was their King, and God they durſt Depoſe.
Urge now your Piety, your Filial Name,
A Father's Right, and Fear of future Fame:
The Publick Good, that Univerſal Call,
To which even Heav'n ſubmitted, anſwers all.
Nor let his Love Enchant your generous Mind;
'Tis Nature's trick to propagate her Kind.
Our fond Begetters, who would never die,
Love but themſelves in their Poſterity
Or let his Kindneſs by th' Effects be try'd,
Or let him lay his vain Pretence aſide.
God ſaid he lov'd your Father; could he bring
A better Proof, than to Anoint him King?
It ſurely ſhew'd he lov'd the Shepherd well,
Who gave ſo fair a Flock as *Iſrael*.
Would *David* have you thought his Darling Son?
What means he then, to Alienate the Crown?
The name of Godly he may bluſh to bear:
'Tis after God's own heart to Cheat his Heir;
He to his Brother gives Supreme Command,
To you a Legacy of Barren Land:
Perhaps th' old Harp on which he thrums his Lays;
Or ſome dull *Hebrew* Ballad in your Praiſe.

B   Then

Then the next Heir, a Prince Severe and Wiſe;
Already looks on you with Jealous Eyes;
Sees through the thin Diſguiſes of your Arts,
And marks the Progreſs in the Peoples Hearts.
Though now his mighty Soul its Grief contains;
He meditates Revenge who leaſt complains.
And like a Lion, Slumb'ring in the way,
Or Sleep diſſembling, while he waits his Prey,
His fearleſs Foes within his diſtance draws;
Conſtrains his Roaring, and contracts his Paws:
Till at the laſt, his time for fury found,
He ſhoots with ſudden Vengeance from the Ground,
The proſtrate vulgar, paſſes o'er, and ſpares,
But with a lordly Rage, his Hunters tears.
Your Caſe no tame expedients will afford.
Reſolve on Death, or Conqueſt by the Sword,
Which for no leſs a ſtake than Life you Draw;
And Self defence is Nature's Eldeſt Law.
Leave the warm People no Conſidering time:
For then Rebellion may be thought a Crime.
Prevail your ſelf of what Occaſion gives,
But try your Title while your Father lives:
And, that your Arms may have a fair pretence,
Proclaim you take them in the King's Defence:
Whoſe Sacred Life each Minute would expoſe,
To Plots, from ſeeming Friends, and ſecret Foes:
And who can ſound the depth of *David's* Soul?
Perhaps his fear, his kindneſs may controul.
He fears his Brother, tho' he loves his Son,
For plighted Vows too late to be undone.
If ſo, by force he wiſhes to be gain'd;
Like Womens Lechery, to ſeem conſtrain'd:

Doubt

Doubt not : but, when he moſt affects the Frown
Commit a pleaſing Rape upon the Crown.
Secure his Perſon to ſecure your Cauſe ;
They who poſſeſs the Prince, poſſeſs the Laws.
   He ſaid, And this Advice above the reſt,
With *Abſalom*'s mild Nature ſuited beſt ;
Unblam'd of Life, (Ambition ſet aſide,)
Not ſtain'd with Cruelty, nor puft with Pride:
How happy had he been, if Deſtiny
Had higher plac'd his Birth, or not ſo high !
His Kingly Virtues might have claim'd a Throne ;
And bleſt all other Countries but his own.
But charming Greatneſs, ſince ſo few refuſe ;
'Tis juſter to Lament him, than Accuſe.
Strong were his hopes a Rival to remove,
With Blandiſhments to gain the publick Love ;
To head the Faction while their Zeal was hot,
And Popularly proſecute the Plot.
To further this *Achitophel* Unites
The Male-contents of all the *Iſraelites* ;
Whoſe differing Parties he could wiſely Joyn,
For ſeveral Ends, to ſerve the ſame Deſign.
The Beſt, and of the Princes ſome were ſuch,
Who thought the pow'r of Monarchy too much :
Miſtaken Men, and Patriots in their Hearts ;
Not Wicked but ſeduc'd by impious Arts.
By theſe the Springs of Property were bent,
And wound ſo high, they crack't the Government.
The next for Intereſt ſought t'embroil the State,
To ſell their Duty at a dearer rate ;
And make their *Jewiſh* Markets of the Throne ;
Pretending publick Good, to ſerve their own.
                       Others

Others thought Kings an uſeleſs heavy Load,
Who Coſt too much, and did too little Good,
Theſe were for laying Honeſt *Davia* by,
On Principles of pure good Husbandry.
With them joyn'd all th' Haranguers of the Throng,
That thought to get Preferment by the Tongue.
Who follow'd next, a double danger bring,
Not only hating *David*, but the King;
The *Solymæan* Rout; well Vers'd of old,
In Godly Faction, and in Treaſon bold;
Cowring and Quaking at a Conqu'ror's Sword,
But Lofty to a Lawful Prince Reſtor'd;
Saw with Diſdain an *Ethnick* Plot begun.
And Scorn'd by *Jebuſites* to be Out-done.
Hot *Levites* Headed theſe; who pull'd before
From th' *Ark*, which in the Judges days they bore,
Reſum'd their Cant, and with a Zealous Cry,
Purſu'd their old belov'd Theocracy.
Where Sanhedrin and Prieſt enſlav'd the Nation;
And juſtify'd their Spoils by Inſpiration:
For who ſo fit for Reign as *Aaron*'s Race,
If once Dominion they could found in Grace?
Theſe led the Pack: though not of ſureſt ſcent,
Yet deepeſt mouth'd againſt the Government.
A numerous Hoſt of dreaming Saints ſucceed;
Of the true old Enthuſiaſtick Breed:
'Gainſt Form and Order they their Pow'r employ;
Nothing to Build, and all things to Deſtroy:
But far more numerous was the Herd of ſuch,
Who think too little, and who talk too much.
Theſe out of mere inſtinct, they knew not why,
Ador'd their Father's God, and Property;

And

And, by the fame blind Benefit of Fate,
The Devil and the *Jebufite* did hate :
Born to be fav'd, even in their own defpight ;
Becaufe they could not help believing right.
Such were the Tools ; but a whole Hydra more
Remains, of fprouting heads too long to fcore.
Some of their Chiefs were Princes of the Land ;
In the firft Rank of thefe did *Zimri* ftand :
A man fo various, that he feem'd to be
Not one, but all Mankind's Epitome.
Stiff in Opinion , always in the wrong ;
Was every thing by Starts, and Nothing long ;
But, in the courfe of one revolving Moon,
Was Chymift, Fidler, Statef-man and Buffoon ;
Then all for Women, Painting, Rhiming, Drinking ;
Befides ten thoufand Freaks that dy'd in thinking
Bleft Madman, who cou'd every hour employ,
With fomething New to wifh, or to enjoy !
Railing and praifing were his ufual Themes ;
And both (to fhew his Judgment) in Extremes :
So over Violent, or over Civil,
That every Man, with him, was God or Devil
In fquandring Wealth was his peculiar Art ;
Nothing went unrewarded, but Defert.
Beggar'd by Fools, whom ftill he found too late :
He had his Jeft, and they had his Eftate,
He laugh'd himfelf from Court ; then fought Relief
By forming Partics, but could ne'er be Chief :
For, fpight of him, the weight of Bufinefs fell
On *Abfalom*, and wife *Achitophel* :
Thus, wicked but in Will, of Means bereft,
He left not Faction, but of That was left.

Title

Titles and Names 'twere tedious to rehearfe
Of Lords, below the dignity of Verfe.   (beſt :
Wits, Warriers, Common-wealths. men, were the
Kind Husbands, and mere Nobles all the reſt.
And therefore, in the name of Dulneſs, be
The well hung *Balaam* and cold *Caleb* free.
And Canting *Nadab* let Oblivion damn,
Who made new Porrage for the Paſchal-Lamb.
Let Friendſhip's holy Band ſome Names aſſure :
Some their own Worth, and ſome let Scorn ſecure.
Nor ſhall the Raſcal Rabble here have Place,
Whom Kings no Titles gave, and God no Grace ;
Not Bull-fac'd *Jonas*, who cou'd Statutes draw
To mean Rebellion, and make Treaſon Law.
But he, though bad, is follow'd by a worſe,(Curſe :
The Wretch, who Heav'ns anointed dai'd to
Shimei, whoſe Youth did early Promiſe bring
Of Zeal to God, and Hatred to his King;
Did wiſely from Expenſive Sins refrain,
And never broke the Sabbath, but for Gain ;
Nor ever was he known an Oath to vent,
Or Curſe, unleſs againſt the Government.
Thus, heaping Wealth, by the moſt ready way
Among the *Jews*, which was to Cheat and Pray ;
The City, to reward his pious Hate
Againſt his Maſter, choſe him Magiſtrate;
His Hand a Vare of Juſtice did uphold ;
His Neck was loaded with a Chain of Gold.
During his Office, Treaſon was no Crime.
The Sons of *Belial* had a Glorious Time ;
For *Shimei*, though not Prodigal of Pelf,
Yet lov'd his wicked Neighbour as himſelf

When

When two or three were gather'd to Declaim
Againſt the Monarch of *Jeruſalem*,
Shimei was alwa)s in the midſt of them.
And, if they Curſt the King when he was by,
Would rather Curſe, than break good Company.
If any durſt his Factious Friends accuſe,
He pact a Jury of Diſſenting *Jews*:
Whoſe fellow-feeling in the Godly Cauſe
Wou'd free the ſuffering Saint from Humane Laws:
For Laws are only made to puniſh thoſe
Who ſerve the King, and to protect his Foes.
If any leiſure time he had from Pow'r,
(Becauſe 'tis Sin to miſ-employ an hour :)
His Buſineſs was by Writing to perſwade,
That Kings were Uſeleſs, and a Clog to Trade:
And, that his noble Style he might refine,
No *Rechabite* more ſhun'd the fumes of Wine.
Chaſt were his Cellars; and his ſhrieval Board
The Groſſneſs of a City Feaſt abhor'd:
His Cooks, with long diſuſe, their Trade forgot:
Cool was his Kitchen, tho' his Brains were hot.
Such frugal Vertue Malice may accuſe;
But ſure 'twas neceſſary to the *Jews*;
For Towns once burnt, ſuch Magiſtrates require,
As dare not tempt God's Providence by Fire.
With Spiritual Food he fed his Servants well,
But free from Fleſh, that made the *Jews* rebel:
And *Moſes*' Laws he held in more Account,
For forty days of faſting in the Mount.
To ſpeak the reſt, who better are forgot,
Would tire a well breath'd Witneſs of the Plot:
Yet, *Corah*, thou ſhalt from Oblivion paſs;
Erect thy ſelf thou Monumental Braſs:

Hi

High as the Serpent of thy Metal made
While Nations ſtand ſecure beneath thy ſhade.
What tho' his Birth were baſe yet Comets riſe
From Earthly Vapours e'er they ſhine in Skies.
Prodigious Actions may as well be done
By Weaver's Iſſue, as by Prince's Son.
This Arch-Atteſtor for the Publick Good,
By that one Deed Enobles all his Blood.
Who ever ask'd the Witneſſes high Race,
Whoſe Oath with Martyrdom did *Stephen* grace?
Ours was a *Levite*, and as times went then,
His Tribe were God Almighty's Gentlemen.
Sunk were his Eyes, his Voice was harſh and loud,
Sure Sign, he neither Cholerick was, nor Proud:
His long Chin prov'd his Wit, his Saint-like Grace,
A Church Vermillion, and a *Moſes'* Face.
His Memory Miraculouſly great,
Cou'd Plots, exceeding Man's belief, repeat,
Which therefore cannot be Accounted Lies,
For Human Wit, cou'd never ſuch deviſe.
Some future Truths are mingled in his Book;
But where the Witneſs fail'd the Prophet ſpoke:
Some things like Viſionary Flights appear;
The Spirit caught him up the Lord knows where:
And gave him his *Rabinical* Degree,
Unknown to Foreign Univerſity
His Judgment yet, his Mem'ry did excel;
Which piec'd his Wond'rous Evidence ſo well:
And Suited to the Temper of the Times;
Then Groaning under *Jebuſitick* Crimes.
Let *Iſrael*'s Foes Suſpect his Heav'nly call,
And raſhly Judge his Wit Apocryphal;

Our

Our Law, for ſuch Affronts have Forfeits made;
He takes his Life, who takes away his Trade.
Were I my ſelf in Witneſs *Corah*'s place,
The Wretch who did me ſuch a dire Diſgrace,
Shou'd Whet my Memory, tho' once forgot,
To make him an Appendix of my Plot.
His Zeal to Heav'n, made him his Prince deſpiſe,
And Load his Perſon with Indignities :
But Zeal peculiar Privilege affords,
Indulging Latitude to Deeds, and Words,
And *Corah* might for *Agag*'s Murther call ;
In Terms as courſe a *Samuel* us'd to *Saul*.
What others in his Evidence did join,
(The beſt that could be had for Love or Coin,)
In *Corah*'s own Predicament will Fall,
For *Witneſs* is a common Name to all.
  Surrounded thus with Friends of every Sort,
Deluded *Abſalom*, forſakes the Court :
Impatient of high Hopes, urg'd with Renown,
And Fir'd with near Poſſeſſion of a Crown.
Th' admiring Croud are dazled with ſurprize,
And on his Goodly Perſon feed their Eyes ;
His joy conceal'd, he ſets himſelf to ſhow :
On each ſide bowing popularly low :
His Looks, his Geſtures, and his Words he frames,
And with familiar eaſe repeats their Names.
Thus form'd by Nature, furniſht out with Arts,
He glides unfelt into their ſecret hearts.
Then, with a kind compaſſionating look,
And ſighs, beſpeaking pity e'er he ſpoke,
Few Words he ſaid ; but eaſie thoſe and fit,
More ſlow than Hybla-drops, and far more ſweet.

I mourn

I mourn, my Country-men, your loſt Eſtate;
Though far unable to prevent your Fate:
Behold a Baniſh'd Man, for your dear Cauſe,
Expos'd a Prey to Arbitrary Laws!
Yet oh ! that I alone cou'd be undone,
Cut off from Empire, and no more a Son!
Now all your Liberties a Spoil are made,
Ægypt and *Tyrus* intercept your Trade,
And *Jebuſites* your Sacred Rites invade.
My Father, whom with Reverence yet I Name,
Charm'd into eaſe, is careleſs of his Fame :
And brib'd with petty Sums of Foreign Gold,
Is grown in *Bathſheba*'s Embraces Old.
Exalts his Enemies, his Friends deſtroys;
And all his Power againſt himſelf Employs.
He gives, and let him give my Right away;
But why ſhou'd he his own, and yours betray?
He only, he can make the Nation bleed,
And he alone from my Revenge is freed.
Take then my Tears (with that he wip'd his Eyes)
'Tis all the Aid my preſent Pow'r Supplies:
No Court Informer can theſe Arms accuſe,
Theſe Arms may Sons againſt their Fathers uſe;
And 'tis my wiſh the next Succeſſor's Reign,
May make no other *Iſraelites* complain.
  Youth, Beauty, Graceful Actions, ſeldom fail;
But Common Intereſt always will prevail:
And pity never ceaſes to be ſhown,
To him, who makes the Peoples wrongs his own.
The Croud, (that ſtill believe their Kings oppreſs,)
With lifted Hands their young *Meſſiah* bleſs.
Who now begins his Progreſs to ordain ;
With Chariots, Horſemen, and a num'rous Train:
From

From Eaſt to Weſt his Glories he diſplays:
And, like the Sun, the promis'd Land Surveys.
Fame runs before him, as the Morning Star;
And Shouts of Joy Salute him from a far:
Each Houſe receives him as a Guardian God;
And Conſecrates the Place of his abode:
But Hoſpitable Treats did moſt commend,
Wiſe *Iſſachar*, his wealthy Weſtern Friend.
This moving Court, that caught the Peoples Eyes,
And ſeem'd but Pomp, did other Ends diſguiſe.
Achitophel had form'd it, with Intent
To Sound the Depths, and Fathom where it went.
The Peoples Hearts; diſtinguiſh Friends from Foes;
And try their Strength, before they came to Blows.
Yet all was colour'd with a ſmooth pretence,
Of Specious Love, and Duty to their Prince.
Religion, and Redreſs of Grievances,
Two Names, that always cheat, and always pleaſe,
Are often urg'd; and good King *David*'s Life,
Endanger'd by a Brother and a Wife.
Thus in a Pageant Shew; a Plot is made;
And Peace it ſelf is War in Maſquerade.
Oh fooliſh *Iſrael*! never warn'd by ill!
Still the ſame bait, and Circumvented ſtill!
Did ever Men forſake their preſent eaſe,
In midſt of Health Imagine a Diſeaſe;
Take pains Contingent miſchiefs to foreſee,
Make Heirs for Monarchs, and for God decree?
What ſhall we think, Can People give away,
Both for themſelves and Sons, their Native Sway?
Then they are left defenceleſs to the Sword
Of each unbounded arbitrary Lord.

And

And Laws are vain, by which we Right enjoy,
If Kings unqueſtion'd can thoſe Laws deſtroy.
Yet if the Crowd be Judge of fit and Juſt,
And Kings are only Officers in Truſt,
Then this reſuming Cov'nant was declar'd
When Kings were made, or is for ever bar'd :
If thoſe who gave the Sceptre cou'd not tie
By their own deed their own Poſterity,
How then cou'd *Adam* bind his future Race ?
How cou'd his forfeit on Mankind take place ?
Or how cou'd Heavenly Juſtice damn us all,
Who ne'er conſented to our Father's Fall ? (mand,
Then Kings are ſlaves to thoſe whom they com-
And Tenants to their People's pleaſure ſtand.
Add, that the Pow'r for Property allow'd.
Is miſchievouſly ſeated in the Croud ;
For who can be ſecure of private Right,
If Sovereign Sway may be diſſolv'd by Might ?
Nor is the Peoples Judgment always true ;
The moſt may err, as groſly as the Few.
And faultleſs Kings run down, by Common Cry.
For Vice, Oppreſſion, and for Tyranny.
What Standard is there in a fickle Rout,
Which flowing to the Mark, runs faſter out ?
Nor only Crowds but Sanhedrins may be
Infected with this Publick Lunacy.
And Share the madneſs of Rebellious Times,
To Murder Monarchs for Imagin'd Crimes.
If they may give and take whene'er they pleaſe,
Not Kings alone, (the God-head Images)
But Government it ſelf at length muſt fall
To Natures State, where all have Right to all.

Yet,

Yet, grant our Lords the People King's can make,
What prudent Men a fettled Throne wou'd fhake?
For whatfoe'er their Sufferings were before,
That Change they Covet makes them fuffer more.
All others Errors but difturb a State;
But Innovation is the Blow of Fate.
If antient Fabricks nod, and threat to fall,
To Patch the Flaws, and Buttrefs of the Wall.
Thus far 'tis Duty; but here fix the Mark;
For all beyond it, is to touch our Ark.
To change Foundations, caft the Frame anew,
Is work for Rebels who bafe Ends purfue:
At once Divine and Human Laws controul;
And mend the Parts by ruine of the Whole.
The tamp'ring World is Subject to this Curfe,
To Phyfick their Difeafe into a Worfe.

   Now what Relief can Righteous *David* bring?
How Fatal 'tis to be too good a King!
Friends he has few, fo high the madnefs grows;
Who dare be fuch, muft be the People's Foes;
Yet fome there were, ev'n in the worft of Days;
Some let me Name, and Naming is to Praife.

   In this fhort File *Barzillai* firft appears;
Barzillai crown'd with Honour and with Years;
Long fince, the rifing Rebels he withftood
In Regions wafte beyond the *Jordan*'s Flood.
Unfortunately brave to buoy the State;
But finking underneath his Mafter's Fate.
In Exile with his God-like Prince he mourn'd;
For him he fuffer'd, and with him Return'd.
The Court he practis'd, not the Courtier's Art;
Large was his Wealth, but larger was his Heart;
                      Which

Which well the nobleſt Objects knew to Chuſe,
The Fighting Warriour, and Recording Muſe.
His Bed could once a fruitful Iſſue boaſt ;
Now more than half a Father's Name is loſt.
His eldeſt hope, with every Grace adorn'd
By me (ſo Heav'n will have it) always mourn'd,
And always Honour'd ſnatch'd in Manhoods Prime,
B' unequal Fates, and Providences Crime ;
Yet not before the Goal of Honour won
All Parts fulfill'd of Subject and a Son.
Swift was the Race, but ſhort the Time to run.
Oh narrow Circle, but of Pow'r Divine,
Scanted in Space, but perfect in thy Line !
By Sea, by Land, thy matchleſs Worth was known,
Arms thy Delight, and War was all thy Own ;
Thy force, infus'd, the fainting *Tyrians* prop'd,
And haughty *Pharoah* found his Fortune ſtop'd.
Oh Ancient Honour, Oh unconquer'd Hand,
Whom Foes unpuniſh'd never cou'd withſtand !
But *Iſrael* was unworthy of his Name ;
Short is the date of all Immoderate Fame.
It looks as Heav'n our Ruine had deſign'd,
And durſt not truſt thy Fortune and thy Mind.
Now free from Earth, thy diſencumbred Soul
Mounts up, and leaves behind the Clouds and Starry
                                          (Pole ;
From thence thy kindred Legions maiſt thou bring,
To Aid the Guardian Angel of thy King.
Here ſtop my Muſe, here ceaſe thy Painful flight,
No Pinions can purſue Immortal height.
Tell good *Barzilai* thou canſt Sing no more,
And tell thy Soul he ſhould have fled before ;
Or fled ſhe with his Life, and left this Verſe
To hang on her departed Patron's Hearſe.   Now

Now take thy ſteepy flight from Heaven, and ſee
If thou canſt find on Earth another He;
Another He would be too hard to find
See then whom thou canſt ſee not far behind.
Zadoc the Prieſt, whom ſhunning Pow'r and Place,
His lowly mind advanc'd to *David's* Grace;
With him the *Sagan* of *Jeruſalem,*
Of hoſpitable Soul and Noble Stem;
His of the Weſtern Dome, whoſe weighty Senſe
Flows in fit Words and Heavenly Eloquence.
The Prophets Sons by ſuch Example led,
To Learning and to Loyalty were bred;
For *Colleges* on bounteous Kings depend,
And never Rebel was to Arts a Friend.
To theſe ſucceed the Pillars of the Laws;
Who beſt cou'd plead and beſt can judge a Cauſe.
Next them a train of Loyal Peers aſcend,
Sharp judging *Adriel,* the Muſes Friend,
Himſelf a Muſe;—In Sanhedrins debate
True to his Prince, but not a Slave of State.
Whom *David's* Love with Honours did adorn,
That from his diſobedient Son were torn.
Jotham of piercing Wit, and pregnant Thought
Endu'd by Nature, and by Learning taught
To move Aſſemblies, who but only try'd
The worſe a-while, then choſe the better ſide.
Nor choſe alone, but turn'd the Ballance too:
So much the weight of one Brave Man can do.
Huſhai the Friend of *David* in diſtreſs,
In publick ſtorms of manly ſtedfaſtneſs;
By Foreign Treaties he inform'd his Youth;
And join'd Experience to his Native Truth,

His

His frugal care ſupply'd the wanting Throne;
Frugal for that, but bounteous of his own.
'Tis eaſie Conduct when Exchequers flow;
But hard the task to manage well the low?
For Sovereign Pow'r is too depreſt or high,
When Kings are forc'd to ſell or Crouds to buy.
Indulge one labour more, my weary Muſe,
For *Amiel*; who can *Amiel's* praiſe refuſe;
Of antient Race by Birth, but nobler yet
In his own worth, and without Title Great.
The Sanhedrin long time as Chief he rul'd,
Their Reaſon guided, and their Paſſion cool'd;
So dextrous was he in the Crown's defence,
So form'd to ſpeak a Loyal Nations Senſe,
That as their Band was *Iſrael's* Tribes in ſmall,
So fit was he to repreſent them all.
Now raſher Charioteers the Seat aſcend,
Whoſe looſe Careers his ſteady Skill commend.
They, like th' unequal Ruler of the Day,
Miſguide the Seaſons, and miſtake the Way;
While he withdrawn at their mad Labour ſmiles,
And ſafe enjoys the Sabbath of his Toils
  Theſe were the chief; a ſmall but faithful Band
Of Worthies, in the Breach who dar'd to ſtand
And tempt th' united Fury of the Land.
With grief they view'd ſuch powerful Engines bent,
To batter down the Lawful Government.
A numerous Faction with pretended frights,
In Sanhedrins to plume the Regal Rights.
The true Succeſſor from the Court remov'd;
The Plot, by hireling Witneſſes, improv'd.
Theſe Ills they ſaw, and as their Duty Bound,
They ſhew'd the King the danger of the Wound;
                                        That

That no Conceſſions from the Throne wou'd pleaſe ;
But Lenitives fomented the Diſeaſe:
That *Abſalom*, ambitious of the Crown,
Was made the Lure to draw the People down :
That falſe *Achitophel*'s pernicious Hate,
Had turn'd the Plot to ruine Church and State :
The Council violent, the Rabble worſe ;
That *Shimei* taught *Jeruſalem* to Curſe.

   With all theſe loads of Injuries oppreſt,
And long revolving in his careful Breaſt
Th' event of things at laſt, his Patience tir'd,
Thus, from his Royal Throne, by Heav'n inſpir'd,
The God-like *David* ſpoke, with awful fear
His Train their Maker in their Maſter hear.

   Thus long have I by Native Mercy ſway'd,
My wrongs diſſembl'd, my Revenge delay'd :
So willing to forgive th' Offending Age;
So much the Father did the King Aſſwage.
But now ſo far my Clemency they ſlight,
Th' Offenders queſtion my Forgiving Right.
That one was made for many, they contend ;
But 'tis to Rule, for that's a Monarch's End
They call my tenderneſs of Blood, my Fear :
Though manly Tempers can the Longeſt bear.
Yet, ſince they will divert my Native courſe,
'Tis time to ſhew I am not good by Force.
Thoſe heap'd Affronts that haughty Subjects bring,
Are Burthens for a Camel, not a King:
Kings are the publick Pillars of the State,
Born to ſuſtain and prop the Nations weight :
If my young *Sampſon* will pretend a Call
To ſhake the Column, let him ſhare the Fall :

                     C   But

But, oh, that yet he would repent and live !
How eaſie 'tis for Parents to forgive !
With how few Tears a Pardon might be won
From Nature, pleading for a Darling Son !
Poor, pittied Youth, by my Paternal care,
Rais'd up to all the height his Frame cou'd bear:
Had God ordain'd his Fate for Empire Born,
He wou'd have given his Soul another turn :
Gull'd with a Patriot's name, whoſe modern Senſe
Is one that wou'd by Law ſupplant his Prince:
The Peoples Brave, the Politicians Tool :
Never was Patriot yet, but was a Fool.
Whence comes it that Religion and the Laws,
Should more be *Abſalom*'s than *David*'s Cauſe?
His old Inſtructor, e'er he loſt his Place,
Was never thought indu'd with ſo much Grace.
Good Heav'ns, how Faction can a Patriot Paint !
My Rebel ever proves my Peoples Saint:
Wou'd *They* impoſe an Heir upon the Throne ?
Let Sanhedrins be taught to give their Own.
A King's at leaſt a part of Government ;
And mine as requiſite as their Conſent:
Without my leave a future King to chooſe,
Infers a Right the Preſent to Depoſe :
True, they petition me t' approve their Choice:
But *Eſau*'s Hands ſuit ill with *Jacob*'s Voice.
My pious Subjects for my Safety pray.
Which to ſecure, they take my Pow'r away,
From Plots and Treaſons Heav'n preſerve my Years,
But ſave me moſt from my Petitioners.
Unſatiate as the barren Womb or Grave ;
God cannot grant ſo much as they can crave.

What

What then is left, but with a jealous Eye
To guard the ſmall Remains of Royalty?
The Law ſhall ſtill direct my peaceful Sway,
And the ſame Law teach Rebels to obey:
Votes ſhall no more Eſtabliſh'd Pow'r controul
Such Votes as make a Part exceed the Whole.
No groundleſs Clamours ſhall my Friends remove,
Nor Crouds have Pow'r to puniſh e'er they prove,
For Gods, and God-like Kings their Care expreſs,
Still to defend their Servants in diſtreſs.
Oh, that my Pow'r to Saving were confin'd!
Why am I forc'd, like Heav'n againſt my mind,
To make Examples of another Kind?
Muſt I at length the Sword of Juſtice draw?
Oh, curs'd Effects of neceſſary Law!
How ill my Fear they by my Mercy ſcan,
Beware the Fury of a Patient Man.
Law they require, let Law then ſhew her Face;
They could not be content to look on Grace
Her hinder Parts, but with a daring Eye
To tempt the Terrour of her Front and Dye,
By their own Arts, 'tis Righteouſly decreed,
Thoſe dire Artificers of Death ſhall bleed.
Againſt themſelves their Witneſſes will ſwear;
'Till Viper-like, their Mother Plot they tear:
And ſuck for Nutriment that bloody Gore
Which was their Principle of Life before.
Their *Belial* with their *Beelzebub* will fight;
Thus on my Foes, my Foes ſhall do me right:
Nor doubt th' Event: for Factious Crouds engag
In their firſt Onſet, all their Brutal Rage,
Then let 'em take an unreſiſted Courſe:
Retire and Traverſe, and Delude their Force:

                                                    Bu

But when they ſtand all Breathleſs, urge the Fight
And riſe upon 'em with redoubled Might ;
For lawful Pow'r is ſtill ſuperiour found,
.When long driven back, at length it ſtand ht e
                                        (ground.

    He ſaid. Th' Almighty nodding gave conſent ;
And Peals of Thunder ſhook the Firmament,
Henceforth a Series of new Time began,
The mighty Years in long Proceſſion ran ;
Once more the God-like *David* was reſtor'd,
And willing Nations knew their lawful Lord.

The KEY.

Abbethdin	L. Chancellor	The Jews	The Engliſh
Abſalom	D. Monmouth	Jonas	Sir W. Jones
Anabel	Dſs. Monm	Jotham	Mar. Halifax
Achitophel	E Shaftsbury	Iſhboſheth	R. Cromwell
Adriel	E. Mulgrave	Iſrael's Mon.	K. Charles 2 d
Auriel	S. Jo Seymor	Iſachar	T. Thin. Eſq;
Barzillai	D. of Ormond	Michal	Q Catherine
Bathſheba	Dſs of Portl	Pharoah	K of France
Corah	Oates	Sagan of Jeru.	Biſh. of Lon
The good old Cauſe }	The round heads Cant.	Sanhedrin	The Parliam
		Saul	Cromwell
Gath	Fland. or Fr.	Shimei	L. M. of Lond.
Godlike David	K. Charles 2 d	Sion	London
Hebron	Scotland	Solymean rout	Mob of Lond
Hot Levites	Prel. Clergy	Theſe Ad. wits	En. Virtuoſi.
Huſhai	E. Ro. & Hyde	The Jewiſh Rabbins }	Engliſh Biſh.
The ſober part of Iſrael }	Of England	The Egypti-an Rites }	Ro. Religion
Old Jeruſalem	London	Zimri	D. Bucking
Jebuſites	Papiſts		

FINIS.

CPSIA information can be obtained
at www.ICGtesting.com
Printed in the USA
LVHW101100020720
659542LV00013B/1577

9 781170 804599